best easy day hikes

Denver

Tracy Salcedo

FALCON®

GUILFORD, CONNECTICUT
AN IMPRINT OF THE GLOBE PEQUOT PRESS

AFALCONGUIDE®

Library of Congress Cataloging-in-Publication Data
Salcedo, Tracy.
    Best easy day hikes, Denver / Tracy Salcedo.
        p. cm.
    ISBN 1-56044-829-6
    1. Hiking--Colorado--Denver Region--Guidebooks. 2. Trails--Colo-
    rado--Denver Region--Guidebooks. 3. Denver Region (Colo.)--Guide-
    books. I. Title.

GV199.42.C62 D477 2000
796.51'09788'83--dc21   00-021982

Manufactured in the United States of America
First edition/Third printing

CAUTION

Outdoor recreational activities are by their very nature potentially hazardous.
All participants in such activities must assume responsibility for their own ac-
tions and safety. The information contained in this guidebook cannot replace
sound judgment and good decision-making skills, which help reduce risk exposure, nor does the scope of this book allow for disclosure of all the potential
hazards and risks involved in such activities.

Learn as much as possible about the outdoor recreational activities in which
you participate, prepare for the unexpected, and be cautious. The reward will be
a safer and more enjoyable experience.

Contents

The Hikes

Dedication
For my sons Jesse, Cruz, and Penn.

Acknowledgments

This book would not have been possible without the help and contributions of a number of people. Thanks to Tripp Addison of Denver Mountain Parks, and Kim Frederick and Kelley Lehman of the Jefferson County Open Space Department, among others, for reviewing portions of the text. Thanks also to George Meyers, the folks at Falcon Publishing, Sandy Weiner, Chris Salcedo, and N. Esser. In addition, thanks are due my hiking partners, including Karen Charland, Molly Garbus, and Sara Bruhl and their families. Most especially, thanks to my sons, Jesse, Cruz, and Penn, and my partner in all things, Martin.

Map Legend

Interstate Highway/Freeway	(00)	Campground	▲
US Highway	(00)	Picnic Area	⊼
State or Other Principal Road	(00) (000)	Building	■
Forest Road	416	Hill/Peak	9,782 ft.
Interstate Highway	⟹	Elevation	9,782 ft. ✕
Paved Road	⟹	River/Creek/ Waterfall	
Gravel Road	⟹	Intermittent Stream	
Unimproved Road	====⟹	Marsh	↯
Trailhead	◯	Gate	•—•
Parking Area	Ⓟ	Bridge/Dam	⏝⏝
Main Trail/Route		Overlook/Point of Interest	◨
Main Trail/Route on Road		National Forest/Park Boundary	
Alternate/Secondary Trail/Route		Cliffs	
Alternate/Secondary Trail/Route on Road		Map Orientation	N
Ski Area Chair Lift	•—•	Scale	0 0.5 1 Miles
City	◯		

Overview Map of Denver

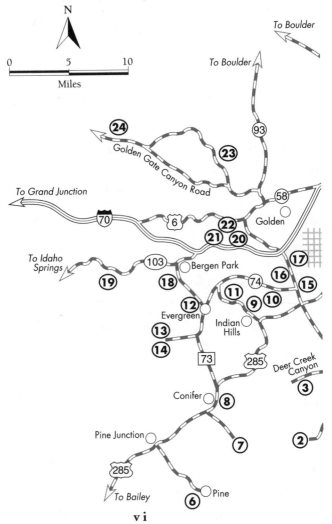

N

0 5 10
Miles

To Boulder

To Boulder

(24)

Golden Gate Canyon Road

(23)

93

58

Golden

To Grand Junction

70

6

(22)

(21) (20)

17

To Idaho Springs

103

Bergen Park

(18)

74

16

15

(19)

(12)

(11)

(9) (10)

Evergreen

Indian Hills

(13)

(14)

73

285

Deer Creek Canyon

(3)

Conifer

(8)

(2)

Pine Junction

(7)

285

To Bailey

(6) Pine

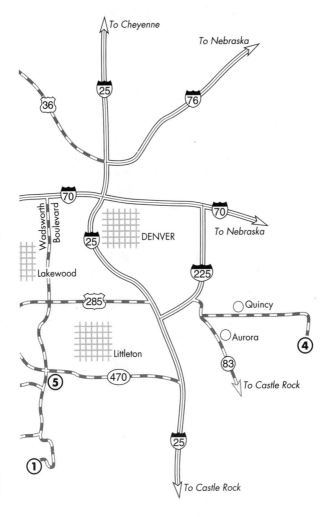

Ranking the Hikes

The following list ranks the hikes in this book from easiest to hardest.

Introduction

The wonder of the foothills that form the backdrop for Denver is their diversity. In some places, dense pine and aspen forests envelope trails in a silent, protective blanket. In other places, the adventurer treads on the exposed and petrified skeleton of the planet. Pictures offer glimpses of this magical landscape, words will inevitably fail to capture it completely. Only by walking through it can anyone fully appreciate its treasures. The hikes in this guide, culled from those included in Chockstone Press's *12 Short Hikes* guidebooks to Denver's foothills, will lead you to some of the best of these mysterious and wonderful places.

The trails discussed within wander among the stunning red-rock towers of Roxborough State Park and Red Rocks Park, along the broad, peaceful shores of the shimmering South Platte River, and to the stark stone ruins of the Walker House atop Mount Falcon. They will lead you to halcyon views atop Chief Mountain, and among the prairie dogs that populate the waving grasses of the high plains. Walk on the wild side; your pleasure is virtually guaranteed.

This is but a small selection of the hikes available in the Denver area, which has been blessed with far-sighted land preservationists including the Jefferson County Open Space Department and the Denver Mountain Parks Department. The success of the work of these organizations, along with many others throughout the state, is testament to the passion of the residents of the Front Range for this unparalleled landscape. I have selected what I consider to be the best short hikes in many open space parks, but these hikes harbor an abundance of other opportunities—enough for a lifetime of exploration.

This guide covers a large area, but the hikes in the foothills can be reached easily by following one of several asphalt threads that connect the Denver metropolitan area to the mountains. In the southern part of the area, U.S. Highway 285 links the foothill communities of Conifer and Aspen Park to the metro area. A number of hikes lie along Colorado 74, which weaves west up Bear Creek Canyon to the community of Evergreen, then arcs north to Interstate 70, the main arterial to the north. A few of the hikes lie north of I-70. While the majority of the hikes are in the foothills, I have also included several hikes on the flatlands to the east.

Easy, of course, is a relative term. Hikes in mountainous areas are going to involve climbing, and some would argue that no hike with inclines and declines is easy. To aid in the selection of a hike that suits particular needs and abilities, I have ranked these hikes from easiest to hardest. Keep in mind that even the steepest of these hikes can be made easy by hiking within your limits and taking rests when you need them.

To determine how long it might take you to complete a hike, consider that on flat ground, most hikers average two miles per hour. Adjust that rate by the difficulty of the terrain and your level of fitness (subtract time if you are an aerobic animal and add time if you are hiking with kids), and you have a ballpark hiking duration. Add more time if you plan to picnic or participate in trailside activities like bird-watching or photography.

—*Tracy Salcedo*

Zero Impact

The trails that weave through the parklands in the foothills west of the Denver metropolitan area are extremely popular, and accommodate an ever-increasing number of visitors. We—as trail users and advocates—must be vigilant that our visits leave no lasting mark.

Trails can accommodate boundless travel if treated with respect. The book *Zero Impact* (Falcon Publishing) is a valuable resource for learning more about these principles.

The Falcon Zero-Impact Principles

- *Leave with everything you brought with you.*
- *Leave no sign of your visit.*
- *Leave the landscape as you found it.*

Litter is unsightly, and potentially dangerous to wildlife. Pack out all your own trash, as well as garbage left by other hikers, including biodegradable items like orange peels and apple cores.

Use outhouses at trailheads or along the trail. There is seldom room nor privacy along these routes for emergency backcountry practices. If you absolutely must go, carry a lightweight trowel so that you can bury your waste 6 to 8 inches deep, and pack out used toilet paper in a plastic bag. Be sure you relieve yourself at least 300 feet away from any wetland, creek, or lake, and well off any established trail.

Stay on established trails. Shortcutting and cutting switchbacks promote erosion. Select durable surfaces, like rocks, logs, or sandy areas, for resting spots. Do not approach or feed any wildlife. Be courteous by not making loud noises while hiking.

Please do not pick flowers, gather plants, or collect insects, rocks, or other artifacts. Leave them for the next hiker to enjoy.

Do not feed the squirrels—they are best able to survive when they are self-reliant, and they are not likely to find snack food along the trail when winter comes.

Many of the trails described herein are also used by horseback riders and mountain bikers. Acquaint yourself with proper trail etiquette and be courteous.

Keep your impact to a minimum by taking only pictures and leaving only footprints. The wildlife and the people who will pass this way another day are thankful for your courtesy.

Play It Safe

Generally, hiking in this area is safe and fun. Still, there is much you can do to ensure each outing is safe and enjoyable. Some suggestions follow, but by no means should this abbreviated list be taken as gospel. I encourage all hikers to verse themselves completely in the science of backcountry travel—it is knowledge worth having and it is easy to acquire. Written material on the subject is plentiful and easy to find through publishers such as Falcon, on the Internet, or through your area outdoors or sporting goods store.

Know the basics of first aid, including how to treat bleeding, bites and stings, and fractures, strains, or sprains. Few of these hikes are so remote that help can not be reached within a short time, but you would be wise to carry and know how to use simple supplies, such as over-the-counter pain relievers, bandages, and ointments. Pack a first-aid kit on each excursion.

Familiarize yourself with the symptoms of altitude sickness, especially if you are visiting the area from a significantly lesser altitude—like sea level. If you or one of your party exhibits any symptom of this potentially fatal affliction, including headache, nausea, and unusual fatigue, head back down. The trail will still be there after you acclimatize.

Know the symptoms of both cold- and heat-related conditions, including hypothermia and heat stroke. The best way to avoid these afflictions is to wear clothing appropriate to the weather conditions, drink lots of water, eat enough to keep the internal fire properly stoked, and keep a pace that is within your physical limits.

Be prepared for the vagaries of Colorado weather. It changes in a heartbeat. The sun can be brutal, so wear sunscreen. Afternoon and evening thunderstorms, while spectacular, harbor a host of potential hazards, including rain, hail, and lightning. Know how to protect yourself. And yes, snow may fall even in summer, so be on guard.

There are ways to deal with the more dangerous critters in the wilds, like mountain lions, bears, and rattlesnakes. Many parks post signs describing useful self-defense tactics should you encounter one of these beasties. Familiarize yourself with the proper etiquette.

Whether short and easy or long and strenuous, you will enjoy each of these hikes much more if you wear good socks and hiking boots. Carry a comfortable backpack loaded with ample water or sport drink, snacks, and/or a lunch, and extra clothing, including a warm hat, gloves, and a jacket. Maps are not necessary, because these trails are short and well-marked, but they are fun to have along. Bring whatever goodies interest you, like a camera, a manual to help you identify wildflowers, binoculars, or a good novel to curl up with on a warm rock.

1
FOUNTAIN VALLEY TRAIL

Type of hike: Loop.
Total distance: 2.2 miles.
Elevation gain: 200 feet.
Maps: USGS Kassler; Roxborough State Park brochure.
Jurisdiction: Roxborough State Park.
Facilities: The park is equipped with restrooms, a visitor center, water (at the visitor center), and 110 parking spaces.
Finding the trailhead: Take Colorado 470 south to the Wadsworth Boulevard exit. Take Wadsworth south 4.2 miles to Waterton Road. Turn left (south) on Waterton, following it for 1.7 miles to Rampart Range Road. Go south (right) on Rampart Range Road for 4 miles to Roxborough Park Road. Go left (south) on Roxborough Park Road, and drive 0.1 mile to the Roxborough State Park entrance. There is a $4 permit fee. No dogs are allowed.

Key points:
0.0 Trailhead.
0.2 Reach the trail fork.
0.5 Pass the Lyons Overlook Trailhead.
1.0 Cross the footbridge.
2.0 Return to the trail fork.

The hike: Roxborough State Park is a showcase for the dusky sawtoothed remnants of an ancient time. Rough, rust-col-

Fountain Valley Trail

To Littleton

Rampart Range Road

Roxborough
Park Road

Persse Place

Lyons Overlook

Fountain Valley Trail

Parking & visitor center

ROXBOROUGH
STATE PARK

South Rim Trail

To Carpenter
Peak

Carpenter
Peak

N

0   0.25   0.5

Miles

ored sentinels of the Fountain Formation jut skyward from the varied landscape at various locations along the Front Range—at the Garden of the Gods in Colorado Springs, in Red Rocks Park in Morrison—but Roxborough is home to a very striking cluster. The ochre expanse of this remarkable geology leans toward the steep backdrop of the Front Range as though it aspires to something higher, a forest of 300-million-year-old rocks that erupts from the oak brush and colorful prairie grasses of the high plains in a grand display.

The Fountain Valley trailhead lies just north of the visitor center. Head north on the trail through scrub oak toward the red rock garden.

Crest a gentle hill and take in the Fountain Valley overlook. The trail forks at the bottom of the hill at the 0.25-mile point; go right (northeast) onto the prairie. Through the gap in the hogback, you can see the high plains. Take in the Lyons Overlook Trailhead (the view is one of the best in the park) on the left (west) at 0.5 mile, and begin a gentle climb.

About 0.2 mile later, the trail drops gently between the hogback and a scrubby hill that hides the red rocks. At the bottom of the hill, pass a resort called Persse Place that consists of a ramshackle corral and recently restored stone house. The trail veers west and up, crossing the creek via a culvert at 1 mile.

Enter the rock garden. A lone cottonwood stands sentinel in the meadow to the right (west) of the trail in front of the George Washington rock. The slope of the path lessens; cross a seasonal stream, and the trail begins to climb again.

At about 1.5 miles, the trail skirts a tall pillar of red rock, passing a bench, then continuing upward. Crest the hill and pass another bench. At 2 miles, reach the fork in the Fountain Valley Trail; go right (south) toward the visitor center (2.2 miles).

Options: Other trails lace through the foothills within the park. The South Rim Trail offers another view of the Fountain Formation, rising almost 300 feet in elevation to allow a birds-eye view of the red rock gardens. Stop at the visitor center for details about this trail and other hiking options.

2
COLORADO TRAIL IN WATERTON CANYON

Type of hike: Out-and-back.
Total distance: 7 miles.
Elevation gain: 80 feet.
Maps: USGS Kassler and Platte Canyon.
Jurisdiction: Waterton Canyon Recreation Area.
Facilities: There is water and a restroom at the trailhead. A picnic area lies about 0.2 mile west of the trailhead.
Finding the trailhead: Take Colorado 470 south to the Wadsworth Boulevard exit. Take Wadsworth Boulevard south for 4.2 miles to Waterton Road. Turn left (south) on Waterton Road, following it 0.2 mile to the parking lot at the trailhead. No dogs are allowed.

Key points:
0.0 Trailhead.
0.5 Head into the canyon.
1.5 Pass the first diversion dam.
2.0 A mine adit lies to the north.
3.5 Reach the Marsten Diversion Dam.

The hike: This immensely popular route winds up Waterton Canyon, following the spectacular South Platte River as it spills westward out of the mountains. The scenic canyon, the rumbling Platte, and the wide, flat trail draws the

Colorado Trail in Waterton Canyon

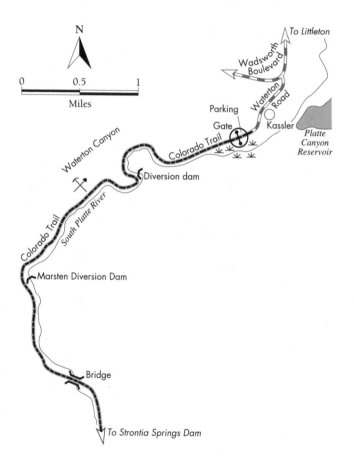

outdoorsy in large but comfortable numbers to the area; hikers share the trail easily with cyclists, equestrians, and families with children in strollers.

The trail leads a double life: Its broad, flat, multi-use surface leads to picnic areas, fishing spots, and seclusion within easy reach of Denver and its suburbs, but it also serves as the eastern terminus for the Colorado Trail, which travels for 473 miles through some of the wildest and most inaccessible country in the Rocky Mountains.

Because the canyon serves as trailhead for a monstrously long walk to Durango, you can hike as far as you please. Limited by length to fit the parameters of an easy day hike, the hike described here takes you about 3.5 miles into the canyon, to the scenic Marsten Diversion Dam and nearby picnic area, but includes time to pause and observe the Rocky Mountain Bighorn sheep that graze along the shores of the Platte in the cooler months. Continue up into the mountains and out into the wilderness if you desire.

To begin, leave the lot on the broad, flat trail/roadway that heads west toward the canyon, passing the restroom and trail sign. The road passes through scrubby and grassy areas, following the South Platte as it winds through shady cottonwoods. A number of picnic areas are scattered riverside.

As the trail curves northwest into the canyon at 0.5 mile, you will see an aqueduct carved into the hillside above the south shore of the river. Pass beneath large water pipes that cross the trail, then by a fishing beach. Beyond, the trail curves westward, arcs beneath impressive cliffs that rise on the right (north) side of the road, then passes the 1-mile marker.

As the trail curves south at about 1.5 miles, pass a small cottonwood-shaded cove on the right (northwest) side of the trail. Rocky Mountain Bighorn sheep frequent this spot in winter. A small diversion dam and a picnic area lie less than 0.25-mile upstream.

The trail curves back west, passes through a concrete "dip," and heads to the 2-mile marker. You can check out a small, closed-up mine adit that plunges into the north canyon wall beyond the marker.

Continue upstream for another mile. At about 3.5 miles, you will reach a second diversion dam, a small residential compound, and a picnic area, then the Marsten Diversion Dam and the broad expanse of river behind the dam. This is the perfect spot to rest, reconnoiter, and enjoy the river before heading back downstream to the trailhead.

Options: Stretch this hike into a vigorous all-day affair, and you can reach spectacular Strontia Springs Dam, which lies 7 miles upstream from the trailhead. Don a backpack and make arrangements for someone to pick you up at another trailhead, and you can follow the Colorado Trail south and west as far as you please. Its western terminus, reached via many a spectacular pass and valley, lies in Durango.

Meadowlark and Plymouth Creek Trails

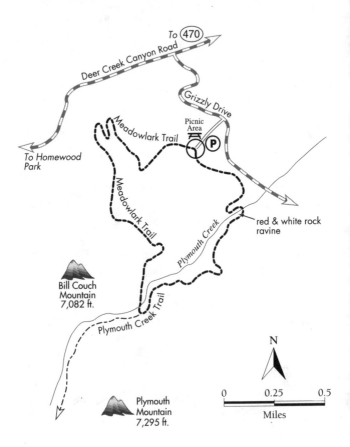

To (470)

Deer Creek Canyon Road

Grizzly Drive

To Homewood Park

Meadowlark Trail

Picnic Area

P

Meadowlark Trail

red & white rock ravine

Plymouth Creek

Bill Couch Mountain 7,082 ft.

Plymouth Creek Trail

Plymouth Mountain 7,295 ft.

N

0   0.25   0.5

Miles

3
MEADOWLARK AND PLYMOUTH CREEK TRAILS

Type of hike: Loop.
Total distance: 3.8 miles.
Elevation gain: 600 feet.
Maps: USGS Indian Hills; Deer Creek Canyon Park brochure.
Jurisdiction: Deer Creek Canyon Park, Jefferson County Open Space Department.
Facilities: You will find restrooms, water, and a telephone at the parking area. Picnic shelters lie north of the parking lot.
Finding the trailhead: Take Colorado 470 south to the Kipling Parkway exit. Go right (south) on Ute for about a quarter of a mile; go right (west) on Owens and follow it for about 3 miles to where it merges into Deer Creek Canyon Road. Follow Deer Creek Canyon Road west for 2.7 miles to Grizzly Drive. Turn left (south) onto Grizzly Drive, and follow it for 0.4 mile to the park entrance.

Key points:
0.0 Trailhead.
1.5 Begin to descend.
2.2 Reach the Plymouth Creek Trail.
2.8 Skirt the red-and-white rock ravine.

The hike: The red-and-white rock of the narrow draw at the end of this hike is the visual and geological highlight of this trail loop. The vivid colors of the rock bands, exposed over time by the mostly placid Plymouth Creek, erupt from the scrubby hillside, snatching the hiker's eye away from the muted greens and yellows of the surrounding sage scrub and prairie grasses and into its depths.

The shallow canyon, however, is not the only thing that will draw your eyes away from the trail. As you climb the Meadowlark Trail, views open into steep, wooded Deer Creek Canyon, and at the hike's apex, you can look east over the hogback to the high plains. Your glance will also be drawn north and south along the expanse of the hogback valley, but don't let the views carry you away, for the rocky and twisting path demands attention.

Begin by leaving the parking lot and going right (north, then west) on the Meadowlark Trail, which climbs up open, grassy slopes that form the foot of the Front Range. Pass through Rattlesnake Gulch, and the trail begins to climb to the first switchback.

Climb another switchback, where views open to the west, up Deer Creek Canyon. Skirt the backside of the scrubby hillock; the trail eventually climbs back to the east-facing slopes. As the trail crosses the southeast face of the mountainside through meadow and scrub oak, you can look across the southern plains and plateaus.

Begin a gentle descent west after about 1.5 miles. Traverse two scrub oak-filled ravines as you descend to a bridge over Plymouth Creek. At the trail intersection at 2.2 miles, go left (east) and downhill on the Plymouth Creek Trail.

Follow the wide trail as it and the stream drop from relatively dense woods onto a scrubby hillside. The trail skirts the south side of the striking red-and-white rock ravine at about 2.8 miles. Three switchbacks lead down into the ravine, where you will cross the creek again. Beyond the creek, the trail aims to the northeast. Follow the rollercoaster path through the scrub back to your car.

4
AURORA RESERVOIR LOOP

Type of hike: Loop.
Total distance: 8.5 miles.
Elevation gain: 50 feet.
Maps: USGS Piney Creek; Aurora Reservoir brochure.
Jurisdiction: City of Aurora.
Facilities: You will find just about everything you need at the trailhead—ample parking, picnic areas, restrooms, a snack bar, and a swimming beach.
Finding the trailhead: To reach the Aurora Reservoir from Interstate 25, take Exit 220/Interstate 225 south. Go 4 miles on I-225 to South Parker Road (Colorado 83). Go right (south) on South Parker Road, and drive 1.8 miles to East Quincy Avenue. Turn left (east) on East Quincy Avenue, and drive 8.2 miles to the park entrance on the right (south). Follow the entrance road for 0.4 mile to the entrance station. A daily vehicle pass is $4; season passes are available. The trailhead is 0.5 mile ahead at the boat ramp parking area.

Key points:
0.8 Cross the small dams.
2.2 Hike around the first inlet.
5.5 Circumnavigate another finger of the reservoir.
6.4 Reach the dam.
7.4 The trail parallels a park road.
8.5 Return to the trailhead.

Aurora Reservoir Loop

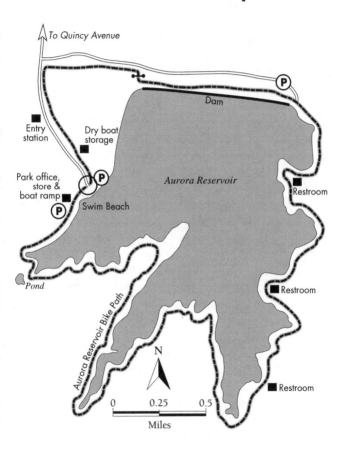

To Quincy Avenue

Entry station

Dry boat storage

Park office, store & boat ramp

Swim Beach

Pond

Aurora Reservoir

Dam

Restroom

Restroom

Restroom

Aurora Reservoir Bike Path

N

0   0.25   0.5

Miles

The hike: Fragrant prairie grasses frame the navy-blue waters of Aurora Reservoir, forming the perfect setting for a splendid day hike. A rolling paved path encircles the reservoir, tracing the long fingers of inlets and reaching into marshlands thick with waterfowl and other wildlife. On the water, the scenery is enlivened by sailboarders and small boats, the sails of which are filled by the sometimes brisk winds that sweep the plains.

Plan to spend the day at the reservoir. After the hike, which qualifies as easy despite its length, enjoy the cooling waters at the swimming beach, fish from the dam, eat lunch or a snack in the picnic area, or, if the wind picks up, try sailing or sailboarding.

To begin the hike, head southwest from the parking lot, walking toward the mountains. Pass the cluster of park buildings (including the restrooms), as well as the swim beach and playground.

At 0.8 mile, you will cross a couple of small dams with a pond on the right (west) side of the trail. Continue on your circuit of the lakeshore, passing a bench overlooking the lake. A workout course parallels the trail.

At 2.2 miles, climb to the summit of a gentle hill for a view of a hidden inlet decorated with sun-bleached snags. Cross the inlet dam and watch for waterfowl in the verdant marsh.

You will circumnavigate another of the reservoir's arms at the 5-mile mark. The distant phalanx of the Front Range forms the western horizon as the trail returns to the main lakeshore. Pass fenced-off solar collectors and a restroom as the trail approaches the dam.

You will reach the reservoir's dam at 6.4 miles. At the intersection with the park service road at the east end of the dam, go left (west), crossing the dam; at its west end, the path veers right (north). Pass through the gate and head down a relatively steep grade to a sharp left (west) turn at the park road. The trail parallels the road as it heads west at 7.4 miles, aiming for the picnic areas and other amenities near the trailhead. Climb the hill to the entry road, and go left (south) on the path, passing the entry station and the dry dock area as you return to the trailhead at 8.5 miles.

5
CHATFIELD RESERVOIR TRAILS

Type of hike: Out-and-back.
Total distance: 6 miles.
Elevation gain: 50 feet.
Maps: USGS Littleton; Chatfield State Park brochure.
Jurisdiction: Chatfield State Park.
Facilities: There is a large parking area at this trailhead. Other facilities, including restrooms, water sources, and picnic areas, as well as marinas, can be found elsewhere in the park.
Finding the trailhead: To reach Chatfield State Park and the trailhead from Colorado 470, take the Wadsworth Boulevard exit. Turn right (south) on Wadsworth and go 0.8 mile to the park entrance road. Go left (east) into the park. A daily pass is $4; season passes are available. Just beyond the entrance station, go right (south and east) for 1.8 miles to the Kingfisher turnoff. Go left (north) on the dirt road into the Kingfisher parking lot.

Key points:
0.5 Pass the campground.
1.6 The pavement ends at the lakeside.
2.0 Pass through the Reservoir Picnic Area.
3.0 Reach trail's end at the Plum Creek Picnic Area.

The hike: The thunderstorms that drench the Front Range on summer afternoons form over the high peaks to the west.

Chatfield Reservoir Trails

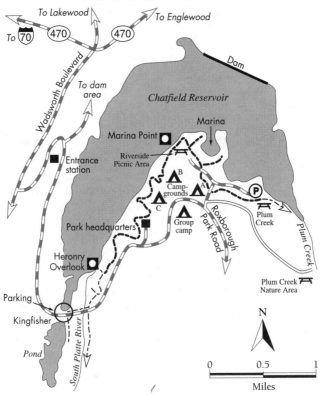

To Lakewood

To Englewood

To 70

470

470

To dam area

Wadsworth Boulevard

Chatfield Reservoir

Dam

Marina

Marina Point

Riverside Picnic Area

Entrance station

B Camp-grounds

A

P

Plum Creek

Plum Creek

Park headquarters

C

Group camp

Roxborough Park Road

Heronry Overlook

Plum Creek Nature Area

Parking

Kingfisher

South Platte River

Pond

N

0   0.5   1

Miles

As clouds are driven eastward by prevailing winds, they become intricate sculptures, pearly white on top and ominously gray below. Chatfield State Park is a great place to watch the development of these thunderheads. Located at the base of the foothills, this park also preserves bottomlands and meadows that harbor a host of flora and fauna. A hike on this gentle trail is a perfect family outing, offering easy walking and the chance to observe both weather and wildlife.

Chatfield Reservoir is open to boating, sailboarding, fishing, and swimming. Dry-land activities include wildlife viewing, picnicking, camping, and a model airplane airway.

Begin by hiking east toward The Heronry overlook. A maze of trails winds through the grasses here; stay right (northwest), circling the observation deck and the north side of the parking lot, to a dirt road. Veer left (northeast) on the paved trail, which parallels the road, and pass park administration and maintenance buildings and a campground at 0.5 mile.

Traverse a section of rough trail as you continue northeast around the reservoir. The paved path meanders from lakeside views to camping areas. At 1.6 miles, the pavement ends at the lakeside. Go right (east) on the wide, dirt track into a riparian area; beyond, the asphalt surface resumes. At the trail intersection near the Riverside picnic shelter, go left (northeast) to the fisherman's point and take in the views. Backtrack to the picnic shelter, cross the road and pick up the trail, which passes restrooms and more picnic tables at 2 miles.

Climb gently to cross another roadway and head toward the camping area. Stay on the asphalt path. Shortly, the trail crosses the road again. Beyond, the pavement is broken as it drops gently into meadowlands at 2.5 miles.

The path melds into the brush along Plum Creek just beyond the secluded Plum Creek picnic area and parking lot at 3.0 miles. If you continue, a dirt footpath leads into the creek area, where you can enjoy the spring and summer blooms amid the cool of the trees. Otherwise, return as you came.

6
NARROW GAUGE TRAIL

Type of hike: Out-and-back.
Total distance: 3 miles.
Elevation gain: 120 feet.
Maps: USGS Pine; Pine Valley Park brochure.
Jurisdiction: Pine Valley Ranch Park, Jefferson County Open Space.
Facilities: There are picnic areas, restrooms, and a water source at the trailhead. Fishing is permitted in the South Platte River and Pine Lake. Fishing piers on the lake are outfitted for persons with disabilities.
Finding the trailhead: From Colorado 470, follow U.S. Highway 285 west 20.8 miles to Pine Junction. Turn left (south) on Jefferson County 126, and go 6 miles to a sharp right turn at the sign for Pine Valley Ranch Park. The park gate is 0.4 mile west.

Key points:
0.0 Trailhead.
0.2 Pass the diversion dam and the Buck Gulch Trail.
0.7 Pass the North Fork View Trail intersection.
1.5 Reach the park's western boundary.

The hike: This peaceful trail follows the North Fork of the South Platte River as it meanders through a stunning valley punctuated by huge, smooth rock outcrops. Perhaps a coy-

Narrow Gauge Trail

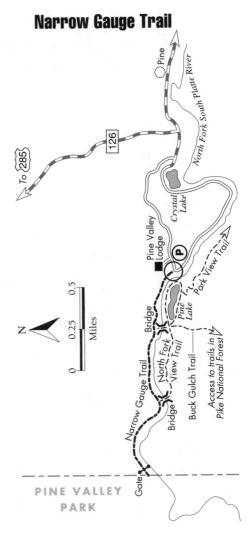

PINE VALLEY PARK

ote will mark your progress from the broad meadow along the river, or elk will gather to feed on the meadow's abundant grasses. Perhaps you will see a hawk scanning the valley floor for prey. Or perhaps you will see no other creature at all, and simply walk in solitude through a landscape sculpted by the Platte.

Pine Valley is not only a natural wonderland. The impressive log-and-stone Pine Valley Lodge once served as a retreat for VIPs visiting Denver. The small manmade lake below the lodge, which is encircled by a trail perfect for beginning hikers, was once a kind of natural refrigerator—large chunks of ice were carved from the pond in winter and shipped by train to Denver to be used in iceboxes.

To begin, head west from the parking area on the wide path. The trail takes you below the northern dike of the lake, then along the willow-choked north shore of the South Platte, gradually veering away from the riverside, then returning to the water near a large pine. As the path leaves the water again, the valley widens and views open of a meadow and large gray rocks that stand sentinel above.

At 0.2 mile, you will reach a diversion dam and trail intersection. The Buck Gulch Trail heads left (south) across the bridge and into the Pike National Forest. Continue straight (west) on the Narrow Gauge Trail.

The trail continues through the meadow, passing beneath a red-rock outcrop. The valley narrows at about 0.7 mile, where another bridge spans the South Platte, leading left (south) to the North Fork View Trail. A rocky, forested wall looms above the river's south shore.

When the valley opens again, the path follows a fenced

property line. At about 1.2 miles, both trail and river curve southward. A huge smooth, gray rock towers above the far (south) shore of the river. At 1.5 miles, you will reach the gate that marks the park boundary – as good a place as any to picnic. Return the way you came.

Options: This park sports 4.6 miles of trail, and provides access to the myriad of opportunities offered by the Pike National Forest. You can add an easy 0.3 mile to the hike by walking around the lake—a perfect jaunt for an adventuresome toddler and his or her family. Check the park map for other short trail loops and links to trails in the Pike National Forest.

7
RAVEN'S ROOST AND OXEN DRAW TRAILS

Type of hike: Loop.
Total distance: 2.5 miles.
Elevation gain: 360 feet.
Maps: USGS Platte Canyon and Pine; Reynolds Park brochure.
Jurisdiction: Reynolds Park, Jefferson County Open Space.
Facilities: Picnic tables and restrooms are at the trailhead.
Finding the trailhead: From its intersection with Colorado 470, follow U.S. Highway 285 west 14 miles to the stoplight in Conifer. Continue west for 0.5 mile on U.S. 285 to Foxton Road. Turn left (south) on Foxton Road (Jefferson County 97) and drive 3.8 miles to the Reynolds Park entrance. Park in the main lot, which is on the left (southwest) side of the road.

Key points:
0.0 Trailhead.
0.3 Begin up the Raven's Roost Trail.
1.0 Check out the views from the Raven's Roost.
1.2 Reach the Oxen Draw Trail.

The hike: The Raven's Roost is a high, rocky point on the slope of a forested mountainside that overlooks a steep, wooded draw. Raven, eagle, or human, the views and exposure of the Roost (not to mention the steep climb up to it)

Raven's Roost and Oxen Draw Trails

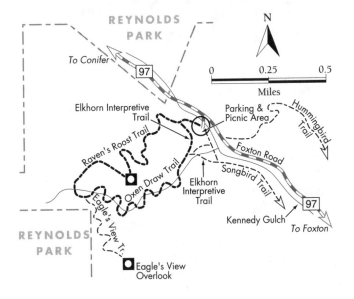

invite you to rest a spell. The draw below is narrow and moist, and the trail through it crosses the seasonal stream time and time again, as though oxen had indeed picked the route.

Like other ranches in the foothills west of Denver, the Reynolds Ranch has an interesting history. For a time, the park was a dude ranch, offering visitors not only the chance to ride horses, fish, and partake of other typical western activities, but they could also play the more civilized game of croquet. The area was also home to the Piano Meadows Mormon settlement, but no traces of this remain.

This is a straightforward hike, a good up-and-downer, mostly under the cover of dense woodland. Choose this hike on a hot summer's day, when the shade of the pines and the winds of the roost can both cool and charm you.

To begin, cross the creek and pass the outhouse, going right (north) on the Elkhorn Interpretive Trail. At the trail fork, go right (northwest), into the meadow. Two switchbacks lead to the head of the meadow, where, at about 0.3 mile, the trail curves west to the Raven's Roost Trail intersection. Continue up and west on the wide Raven's Roost Trail.

The route climbs four broad switchbacks through the forest, flattens briefly, then begins to climb again. Pass a spur trail, and stay left (down and west) on Raven's Roost Trail. At about 1 mile, the ponderosa pines part to reveal the roost, a striking rock outcrop overlooking the wooded draw to the south.

The trail continues by dropping into the ravine. Round a switchback and cross the creek to the intersection with the Oxen Draw Trail and the Eagle's View Trail at about 1.2 miles. Go left (east), and downstream on the Oxen Draw Trail.

The trail fords the creek seven times before passing beneath a rock outcrop. Cross a rock footbridge, then ford the creek four more times. Finally, the trail veers away from the waterway and toward the mouth of the ravine, which ends at the Elkhorn Interpretive Trail at about 1.8 miles. Go right (eastward) on Elkhorn; at the second trail intersection, bear left (eastward again), and cross the stream. The trail wanders another 0.2 mile back to the outhouse and parking lot.

8
LODGEPOLE AND
SUNNY ASPEN TRAILS

Type of hike: Lollipop loop.
Total distance: 2.8 miles.
Elevation gain: 450 feet.
Maps: USGS Conifer; Meyer Ranch Park brochure.
Jurisdiction: Meyer Ranch Park, Jefferson County Open Space.
Facilities: There are restrooms, picnic tables, and a water source available along the Owl's Perch Trail.
Finding the trailhead: From Colorado 470, follow U.S. Highway 285 west for 11.5 miles to its intersection with South Turkey Creek Road. Turn left (south) on South Turkey Creek; the entrance to the park is about 100 yards down the road on the right (south).

Key points:
0.0 Trailhead.
0.6 Reach the Lodgepole Loop Trail.
1.2 Head up on the Sunny Aspen Trail.
1.5 Pass the Old Ski Run Trail intersection.
2.2 Return to the Owl's Perch Trail.

The hike: This loop wanders through the forests of a history-rich former ranch. The remnants of an old ski area, used in the 1940s, are hidden in the upper reaches of the park. And

Lodgepole and Sunny Aspen Trails

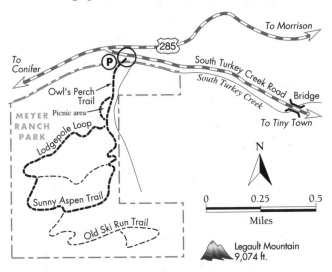

rumor has it P. T. Barnum (of Barnum & Bailey circus fame) housed his animals at the ranch during several winters in the late 1880s.

Don't expect to come across any unusual wildlife forms as you hike this route—instead of elephants and lions, the park is inhabited by the usual assortment of tassel-eared Abert's squirrels, mule deer, and an occasional elk. You will gain a bit of altitude, and so earn views across the scenic Turkey Creek corridor. But it is the forests that give this hike its distinctive flavor, from the quiet envelope of the lodgepole pine woodland to the chattering openness of the old-growth aspen at the trail's apex.

To begin this hike, leave the parking area to the south, following Owl's Perch Trail. Cross the stream and the broad meadow, then climb out of the grass and go right (south) to the wooded picnic area. The trail forks after 0.4 mile; go right (west), and follow the path as it climbs south.

You will reach the Lodgepole Loop Trail at 0.6 mile; turn right (west). Follow the arrows to stay on the trail; the green dots mark cross-country ski routes. Head downhill, passing a covered bench. When the trail crosses the ski route again, stay straight (westward) on the main route.

Round a switchback through the lodgepole forest, and climb to the Sunny Aspen Trail intersection at 1.2 miles. Take the Sunny Aspen Trail to the right (west), starting up the steepest part of the hike.

The climb ends at the Old Ski Run Trail intersection at 1.5 miles. A stone picnic shelter is to the left (north). Continue straight (east) on the Sunny Aspen Trail, heading down through the old-growth aspen for which the trail is named.

A series of switchbacks leads down to the Lodgepole Loop Trail at 2 miles. Go right (north) on Lodgepole, passing three switchbacks as you descend north toward the meadow again. You will come to the Owl's Perch Trail crossing at 2.2 miles; turn right (north) and take the Owl's Perch Trail through the picnic area back to the car.

Options: You can lengthen this loop by adding the 2-mile lollipop loop Old Ski Run Trail, which branches off the Sunny Aspen Trail at the 1.5-mile mark, or you can shorten it by about 0.4 mile by sticking with the Lodgepole Loop Trail.

9
CASTLE AND TOWER TRAILS

Type of hike: Lollipop loop.
Total distance: 2 miles.
Elevation gain: 200 feet.
Maps: USGS Morrison: Mount Falcon Park brochure.
Jurisdiction: Mount Falcon Park, Jefferson County Open Space.
Facilities: The dirt parking area features picnic tables, a water source, and restrooms.
Finding the trailhead: To reach the west parking area of Mount Falcon Park from Colorado 470, follow U.S. Highway 285 south (though it's more west at this point) for 4.1 miles to its intersection with Parmalee Gulch Road. Go right (north) on Parmalee Gulch Road for 2.8 miles to Picutis Road. Picutis is a winding but well-maintained and well-signed dirt road that links into Mount Falcon Road, which deadends in the west parking lot. The parking lot is about 2 miles east of Parmalee Gulch Road.

Key points:
0.0 Trailhead.
0.7 Reach the trail to the Walker ruins.
1.0 Head up the Tower Trail.
1.3 Reach the Tower Lookout.
1.5 Arrive at the Eagle Eye Shelter.

Castle and Tower Trails

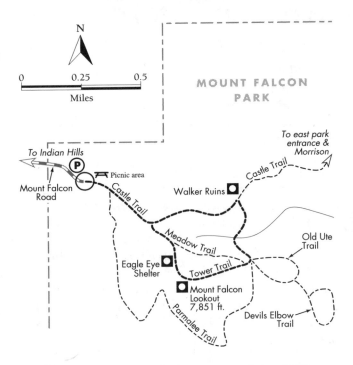

N

0   0.25   0.5
Miles

MOUNT FALCON
PARK

To east park
entrance &
Morrison

To Indian Hills

Mount Falcon
Road

Picnic area

Castle Trail

Castle Trail

Walker Ruins

Meadow Trail

Old Ute
Trail

Eagle Eye
Shelter

Tower Trail

Mount Falcon
Lookout
7,851 ft.

Parmalee Trail

Devils Elbow
Trail

The hike: Mount Falcon Park was part of the 4,000-acre mountain estate of wealthy turn-of-the-century business-man John Brisben Walker. The trail takes you to the site of the magnificent mansion he built on a ponderosa-forested point overlooking the high plains. The house burned in 1918; its stone remnants are a haunting reminder of Walker's ambition. Further east are the skeletal remains of a summer

White House Walker planned to build for U.S. presidents. It was never completed.

This hike also takes you to two lookouts. The Tower, atop Mt. Falcon itself, affords great views of the plains to the east, and the Eagle Eye Shelter offers wonderful views west to towering Mount Evans.

From the parking area, pass through the gate and head southeast on the Castle Trail. Pass the Parmalee trailhead on the right (west) at about 0.1 mile, and continue straight (southeast) on the Castle Trail, which climbs to a trail crossing at the head of the meadow at 0.3 mile. Go left (east) on Castle Trail.

The path drops through the broad meadow—which displays a vigorous bloom of wildflowers in June and July— then enters a ponderosa forest. Reach a triple trail crossing at 0.7 mile. The ruins of the Walker home lie about 100 yards down the path to the left (north).

After visiting the ruins, return to the trail intersection and go left (south) on the Meadow Trail. Enter the meadow and cross a small footbridge; beyond, the trail begins to climb.

At 1 mile, you will reach the intersection of the Meadow Trail with the Parmalee and Old Ute trails. Stay on the Meadow Trail, heading west to the Tower Trail intersection. Go up and southeast on the Tower Trail.

Climb three quick switchbacks. The trail passes a trail marker that points right (north). Cross a flat area, arc to the east, then head north again to the Tower Lookout at about 1.3 miles.

Enjoy views south into the wooded Turkey Creek Canyon, and east onto the high plains, then pick up the trail as it descends. Three flights of stone stairs drop to a trail crossing; go left (north). Pass a horse trail marker, continuing north on the Tower Trail, which leads down to the Eagle Eye Shelter at about 1.5 miles. From this overlook, views are to the west, where Mount Evans, at more than 14,000 feet, dominates the horizon.

From the Eagle Eye Shelter, the trail descends to the right (north) to its western intersection with the Meadow Trail. Go straight (northwest) on Meadow Trail to the Castle Trail crossing; you will head left (northwest) on the Castle Trail to return to the parking area at 2 miles.

Options: More than 11 miles of trail weave through Mount Falcon Park. From the west trailhead and parking area, you can also make a loop on the Parmalee Trail, which leads 2.7 miles through different ecosystems, including a section of trail that was ravaged by fire in the early 1990s. On the east side, you can climb about 3 miles along the steep Turkey Trot and Castle Trails, which feature great views eastward and challenging hiking.

10
CREEKSIDE TRAIL TO THE CASTLE

Type of hike: Out-and-back.
Total distance: 2.6 miles.
Elevation gain: Minimal.
Maps: USGS Evergreen; Lair O' The Bear Park brochure.
Jurisdiction: Lair O' The Bear Park, Jefferson County Open Space Department.
Facilities: There are picnic areas, a water source, and restrooms near the trailhead. A fishing platform accessible to persons with disabilities is along the creek near the parking area.
Finding the trailhead: To reach Lair O' The Bear Park, take Colorado 470 to the Morrison Road/Colorado 8 exit. Take Colorado 8 west through Morrison to the second stoplight. Go straight (west) on Colorado 74, traveling 4.7 miles through scenic Bear Creek Canyon. The park is on the south (left) side of the highway.

Key points:
0.0 Trailhead.
0.3 Reach the first trail fork.
0.8 Cross the bridge spanning Bear Creek.
1.5 Arrive at trail's end.

The hike: The seasons paint the Bear Creek Canyon in vivid and spectacular shades. In autumn, the cottonwoods, willows, and box elders that line Bear Creek erupt in yellow and or-

Creekside Trail to the Castle

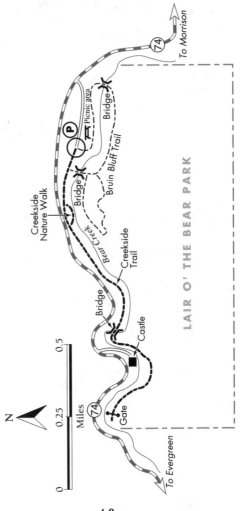

ange, a veritable leafy volcano. In winter, the landscape is silver and brown above its blanket of snow, the creek an inky swath. In spring and summer, nourished by snowmelt and thunderstorms, an expansive array of wildflowers bloom, streaking streamside grasses with the vibrant hues of a Monet painting.

This trail follows lively Bear Creek from the meadows of the eastern part of the park to the narrowing canyon on its western edge, where you can look across the creek at a waterwheel and "castle," on private property.

The trail begins at the west end of the large parking lot. Pass the gate, and ramble down the broad, flat path. Stay straight (right/west) past the bridge spanning Bear Creek on the left (south).

At 0.3 mile the trail forks. You can walk either route—they merge after 0.25 mile—but I recommend you take the left (streamside) course. This, the Creekside Nature Walk, is a narrow footpath that stays close to the waterway. Merge back onto the Creekside Trail at 0.5 mile, and continue left (west).

The route traces Bear Creek to a bridge at 0.8 mile. In early season, when the creek is swollen with meltwater, it flows as a brown vortex of noise and power. In late summer, the water under the bridge is placid and green, bordered by sun-splashed rocks.

The trail narrows as the canyon walls steepen. Pass a private bridge and gaze across the stream at the "castle" and waterwheel. The canyon widens, allowing for a narrow trailside meadow near the trail's end at 1.5 miles. Turn around at the sign and gate blocking a bridge, and return as you came.

O'Fallon Park Upper Loop

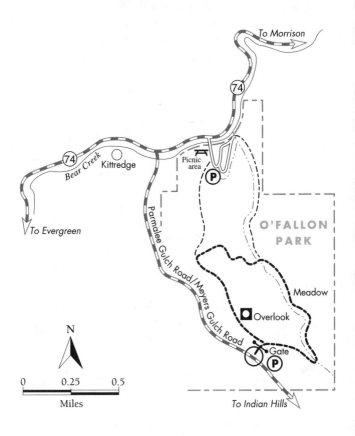

11

O'FALLON PARK UPPER LOOP

Type of hike: Loop.
Total distance: 2.5 miles.
Elevation gain: 200 feet.
Map: USGS Evergreen.
Jurisdiction: O'Fallon Park, Denver Mountain Parks.
Facilities: There are no facilities at the trailhead, but there are restrooms and picnic benches at the park's main entrance, which is located off of Colorado 74 about one-half mile east of its intersection with Parmalee Gulch Road. You can also access this loop from the rear-most picnic area in the lower portion of the park, off Colorado 74. At the time of this writing, Denver Mountain Parks is planning an extensive rehabilitation program for the trail network in the park, as well as at neighboring Corwina Park.
Finding the trailhead: To reach O'Fallon, take Colorado 470 to the Morrison Road/Colorado 8 exit. Follow CO 8 west through Morrison, then continue up Bear Creek Canyon on Colorado 74. Follow CO 74 for 7.9 miles to Parmalee Gulch Road/ Meyers Gulch Road in Kittredge; turn left (south) on Parmalee Gulch Road. Follow the road 1.4 miles to a turnout on the left (east). A chain across a dirt road marks the trailhead. There is limited parking at this site, and very limited parking along the side of Parmalee Gulch Road.

Key points:
0.0 Trailhead.
0.5 Swing through the head of the meadow.
0.7 Reach the trail fork.
1.0 Crest the hill.
2.0 Reach the overlook.

The hike: Hiking in O'Fallon Park is ideal for the time-pressed loner. The park is rustic and scenic—as close as you will get to the backcountry this close to the Denver metropolitan area. There are no trail markers, bathrooms, or picnic tables at this trailhead, and the paths are maintained by the trampling feet of local hikers, their dogs, and the resident wildlife.

Often overlooked by Front Range residents, O'Fallon is never swamped by hikers, even on busy weekends. All the better to enjoy the broad meadow, overgrown with wildflowers in spring, the willow-choked stream that runs trailside for a short distance, and the views of Mount Evans glimpsed through the trees after the rocky climb to the trail's apex. The park is set aside for hikers only.

The trail begins by heading east, around the gate and up the dirt road. At the crest of the hill you will reach a trail intersection. Go straight (east) on the road, through a stand of ponderosa pine, and begin a short descent into a large meadow.

Meander southeast through the flowers; the road swings around the head of the meadow and drops gently northward along its eastern flank at about the 0.5-mile mark.

The road becomes more overgrown as it skirts a willowy creek and drops into a gully. At the trail fork at about 0.7 mile, go left (northwest) over the creek.

Now on a rougher roadbed, you will climb to the crest of the hill at about 1 mile. The route curves to the west, then ascends a short, steep section. Once atop this climb, the trail flattens and traverses the top of a grassy knoll.

The next portion of the trail is intersected by several narrower paths, and can be a bit confusing to the first-time visitor. Remember that you want to circle south and west to complete the loop; if you begin to drop to the east, you will end up in the Bear Creek corridor. At the first intersection, stay left (north) on the path most traveled, and climb to the crest of a wooded hill. At this point, keep left (south). The trail continues up along the forested shoulder of a hillside. This is a steep, rocky climb, but you are rewarded at the top, where a small flat overlook at about 2 miles offers views west of the snowy flanks of Mount Evans.

From the overlook, head downhill to the trail crossing near the stand of ponderosa that you passed near the trailhead. Go right (west) down the road to the parking area and trailhead.

12
EVERGREEN LAKE TRAIL

Type of hike: Loop.
Total distance: 1 mile.
Elevation gain: 40 feet.
Map: USGS Evergreen.
Jurisdiction: Dedisse Park, Denver Mountain Parks; managed by the Evergreen Park and Recreation District.
Facilities: A wonderful recreation facility, the Evergreen Lake House, is located at the trailhead. You will find water and restrooms here—and a whole lot more. In summer, the Evergreen Park and Recreation District rents canoes, and in the winter, once the lake freezes, ice skate rentals are available.
Finding the trailhead: To reach Evergreen Lake, take Colorado 470 south to the Morrison Road/Colorado 8 exit. Follow CO 8 west through Morrison, then continue west on Colorado 74. Follow CO 74 for 10.5 miles through Bear Creek Canyon to downtown Evergreen. Continue through the town, and past the single stoplight, to the road fork at Upper Bear Creek Road (11.1 miles). Go left (west) on Upper Bear Creek Road, and follow it 0.3 mile to the entrance to Evergreen Lake.

Key points:
0.0 Trailhead.
0.5 Reach the base of the spillway.

Evergreen Lake Trail

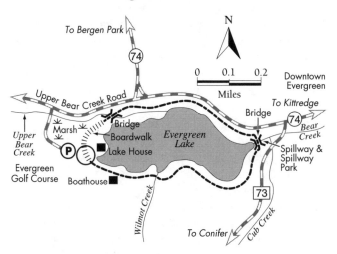

0.7 Skirt the south shore of the lake.
1.0 Pass the boathouse.

The hike: This lovely manmade lake is the heart of the mountain hamlet of Evergreen. The trail that circles the lake is a mirror of the town itself—it is urban and rural, conventional and unusual, polished and rustic, and altogether pleasing.

The beautiful log building at the west end of the lake serves as a warming house for ice skaters in winter and as a boathouse in summer, so you can add water fun to your dryland adventure if you so choose.

The trail leaves the parking lot to the left (northwest), near the main doors of the lake house. Follow the boardwalk north through the wetlands. When you reach Upper Bear Creek, cross a footbridge, then go right (east) on a narrow path through willows. Cross a second footbridge; beyond, the trail is wedged between Upper Bear Creek Road and the creek.

Head right (east), passing a stone wall, to a trail fork. Take the upper route, which follows Colorado 74 to the dam at the east end of the lake. The lower route is an angler's path. This stretch is a bit enervating, as it is separated from the highway only by a metal fence, but it soon ends at the northern abutment of the dam. Cross the abutment, and go down the stairs to the park at the foot of the spillway at about 0.5 mile.

Three footbridges span ribbons of creek in the spillway park. After cooling down in the spray of the artificial waterfall, mount the stairs on the south side of the dam to lakeside. The trail continues west along the south shore of the lake.

At about 0.7 mile, you will reach the first of several forks in the trail. Always stay right, at lakeside; the leftward paths offer access to residents living along the lake. The narrow footpath weaves among the grasses along the lakeshore, occasionally crossing boardwalks and spur trails that lead to small points where anglers try their luck. Views open to the west, up the Upper Bear Creek corridor toward Mount Evans.

At about 0.9 mile, you will cross another footbridge; beyond, the trail forks. Go left (southwest) and climb onto the bluff above the lake, adjacent to the Evergreen Golf Course. Beyond, the trail drops down steps to the historic boathouse at about 1 mile. From here, follow the boardwalk back to the lake house.

13
PONDEROSA AND SISTERS TRAIL LOOP

Type of hike: Loop.
Total distance: 4 miles.
Elevation gain: 200 feet.
Maps: USGS Evergreen and Conifer; Alderfer/Three Sisters Park brochure.
Jurisdiction: Alderfer/Three Sisters Park, Jefferson County Open Space.
Facilities: At the main park entrance, you will find ample parking, restrooms, picnic areas, and the historic Alderfer ranch house. There are also facilities at a second, much smaller parking area located about 1 mile east of the main lot on Buffalo Park Road.
Finding the trailhead: Take Interstate 70 west to the Evergreen Parkway/Colorado Highway 74 exit (Exit 252). Follow Evergreen Parkway south and east for 10 miles to the stoplight in downtown Evergreen and the intersection with Jefferson County Road 73. Turn right (south) on CR 73, and go 0.6 mile to Buffalo Park Road. Turn right (west) on Buffalo Park Road and go 2.3 miles to the park's westernmost parking area.

Key points:
0.0 Trailhead.
0.4 Reach the Ponderosa Trail.

Ponderosa and Sisters Trail Loop
Evergreen Mountain Loop

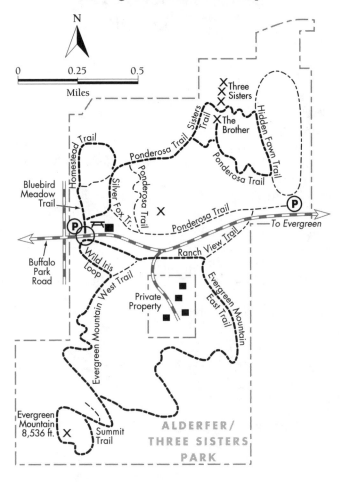

0.9 Head up to the rock formations on the Sisters Trail.
1.6 Drop to the Hidden Fawn Trail.
2.2 Visit the Brother.
3.4 Begin the Homestead Trail.

The hike: Alderfer/Three Sisters is an out-of-the-way gem of a mountain park. The trees are responsible for the marvelous feel of Alderfer—the stately and sweet-smelling ponderosa pines are far enough apart to allow generous sunlight onto the woodland floor, yet close enough to impart a sheltered, protected feel. The dusty summits of the Three Sisters, jumbled rock formations that give the park its name, jut above the forest, and wildflowers spill down their sunny east-facing slopes. Views to the west are of Mount Evans, snowcapped in spring and early summer, muted green and brown in late summer and autumn. To all this, add a quaint farmhouse, a rustic barn, and meadows lush with springtime blooms of purple wild iris...It is simply perfect.

To begin the loop, hike east from the parking lot on the Bluebird Meadow Trail, which curves eastward to a trail intersection with the Silver Fox Trail at 0.1 mile. Head left (north) on the Silver Fox Trail to the first Homestead Trail crossing at 0.2 mile. Stay on Silver Fox past a second intersection with the Homestead Trail; as the path curves northeast through meadows, the Sisters come into view.

You will reach the Ponderosa Trail at 0.4 mile. Go left (northeast) on Ponderosa Trail, abandoning meadow for pine and aspen forests. The Ponderosa Trail leads gently upward to the Sisters Trail at 0.9 mile. Go left (north) on Sisters Trail.

Three switchbacks lead up the steep slope between the

second and third Sisters to the saddle that separates them. If you are a rock climber or confident and skilled scrambler, you can climb onto the Sisters; the climbing is not technical, but does require care.

The trail passes between the formations, then descends six rocky switchbacks on the exposed east side of the Sisters. Reach an intersection with the Hidden Fawn Trail at the base of the ridge at 1.6 miles. Go right (south) on the Sisters Trail.

At 1.9 miles, you will reach the Ponderosa Trail again. Go up and right (west) on the Ponderosa Trail, climbing three switchbacks to the intersection with the Brothers Lookout Trail at 2.2 miles. This 0.2-mile spur leads to a rock outcrop with great views to the east, south, and west. After visiting the Brother, return to the Ponderosa Trail (2.6 miles). Hike another 0.1 mile to the intersection of the Sisters and Ponderosa Trails. Turn left (west), and retrace your steps to the Silver Fox Trail at 3.3 miles.

Add a touch of variety to the final leg of the hike by taking the Silver Fox Trail west for 0.1 mile to the Homestead Trail, then heading right (northwest) on the Homestead Trail, following it around the north side of yet another cool rock formation. The original homestead on the Alderfer property was on the south side of this formation, but very little remains of the structures that once stood here.

You will reach the Bluebird Meadow Trail at 3.8 miles. Follow this through the spectacular meadow, taking care to remain on the trail, which is raised in areas to protect the fragile and marshy ecosystem, and head back to the parking lot and trailhead.

14
EVERGREEN MOUNTAIN LOOP

see map page 50

Type of hike: Loop.
Total distance: 5.5 miles.
Elevation gain: 640 feet.
Maps: USGS Conifer; Alderfer/Three Sisters Park brochure.
Jurisdiction: Alderfer/Three Sisters Park, Jefferson County Open Space.
Facilities: At the main park entrance, you will find ample parking, restrooms, picnic areas, and the historic Alderfer ranch house. There are also facilities at a second, much smaller parking area located about 1 mile east of the main lot on Buffalo Park Road.
Finding the trailhead: Take Interstate 70 west to the Evergreen Parkway/Colorado Highway 74 exit (Exit 252). Follow Evergreen Parkway south and east for 10 miles to the stoplight in downtown Evergreen and the intersection with Jefferson County Road 73. Turn right (south) on CR 73, and go 0.6 mile to Buffalo Park Road. Turn right (west) on Buffalo Park Road and go 2.3 miles to the park's westernmost parking area.

Key points:
0.0 Trailhead.
0.3 Reach the Evergreen Mountain West Trail.
1.8 Three trails meet; head up on the Summit Trail.

3.2 Complete the circuit of the summit.
4.8 Bottom out at the Ranch View Trail.
5.3 Reach the Wild Iris Loop in the meadow.

The hike: Compared with Mount Evans, which rises more than 14,000 feet to the west, Evergreen Mountain is but a well-treed nubbin of a foothill. Regardless, it is a nubbin well-worth exploring. A wide, well-maintained trail wanders along the mountain's north face, through a thick forest of lodgepole pine that resounds with silence. The dense canopy of trees is like a green parasol, sheltering the forest floor from the bright Colorado sun and insulating you from the surrounding vistas until trail's end. There, from a prominent rock outcrop that faces west, you are treated to a panorama that includes the barren heights of Mount Evans, and the rosy summits of the Three Sisters.

Begin by heading south out of the parking lot. Carefully cross Buffalo Park Road to the south meadow, and go right (west) on the Wild Iris Loop. In June, this meadow is often thick with the blooms of its namesake, ranging in color from deep purple to feathery white.

At 0.3 mile, you will reach the Evergreen Mountain West Trail on the border of the forest. Go right (southwest) on Evergreen Mountain West Trail, which climbs into the thick trees. As the trail gently ascends, you will cross several shallow gullies and round five broad, sloping switchbacks. The lodgepole pines are thick and sheltering here, evocative of elves and fairies and other woodland creatures of myth. You may also see creatures of reality, including the busy, tasseleared Abert's squirrel.

At 1.8 miles, you will reach the intersection of the Evergreen Mountain West, Evergreen Mountain East, and Summit trails. Go up and right (southeast) on the Summit Trail, which soon breaks out of the trees on rockier terrain that offers views east of the wooded foothills of Evergreen. Round a sharp switchback and continue climbing to the summit rock outcrop, from which you can ogle Mount Evans and the Three Sisters.

The Summit Trail circles the mostly forested top of the mountain, then heads back down to its intersection with the Evergreen Mountain West and East trails at 3.2 miles. Go right (east) on Evergreen Mountain East Trail.

This stretch of trail is not as forested as the north slope of Evergreen Mountain; instead it passes through a mixed forest of ponderosa, fir, and blue spruce trees that is broken with brief swatches of meadow. Pass a rocky overlook, then broad switchbacks ease the descent. As the trail flattens near the base of the mountain, and in the shadow of private homes, you will meander through a lovely meadow and an aspen grove.

At 4.8 miles, reach the Ranch View Trail. Go left (west) on Ranch View, which climbs across a paved road and then up four steep switchbacks to the edge of the meadow near the trailhead. The Ranch View Trail ends on the Wild Iris Loop at 5.3 miles. A brief, flat stretch leads through the meadow grasses to Buffalo Park Road and the parking lot at 5.5 miles.

Bear Creek Lake Trail Loop

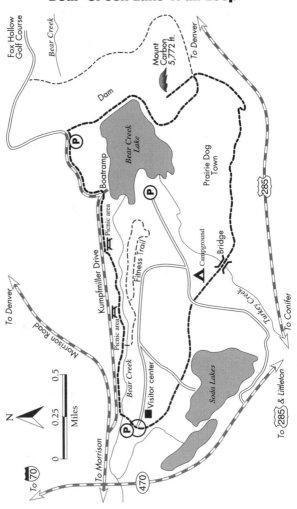

15
BEAR CREEK LAKE TRAIL LOOP

Type of hike: Loop.
Total distance: 8 miles.
Elevation gain: 210 feet.
Maps: USGS Morrison, Bear Creek Lake Park brochure.
Jurisdiction: Bear Creek Lake Park, City of Lakewood.
Facilities: At the trailhead, you will find plenty of parking. In other areas of the park, there are restrooms, water sources, picnic areas, and marinas at both Bear Creek Lake and Soda Lakes.
Finding the trailhead: Take Interstate 70 to the Colorado 470 exit. Follow CO 470 south for 4.5 miles to the Morrison Road/Colorado 8 exit. Go left (east) on Morrison Road, passing under the freeway, to the park entrance on the right (south) side of the road. There is a small fee payable at the gatehouse. Take the first right (south) turn beyond the kiosk. The trail begins at the west end of the Skunk Hollow parking lot.

Key points:
0.7 Reach the intersection with the road to Soda Lakes.
1.4 Pass the picnic and camping areas.
2.6 Walk through the prairie dog town.
3.5 Reach the summit of Mount Carbon.
4.4 Drop to the dam below Bear Creek Lake.
5.0 Climb to the Mountain View parking area.

The hike: An incredible prairie dog colony is the unusual high-light of this great trail loop. The broad concrete path winds up through the open meadowland that is home to these small brown critters, who assume frozen poses as hikers and cy-clists pass, looking much like short hairy pillars of dirt mounted on crumbling brown pedestals. They don't budge, instead furtively watching the flurry of exercise that sur-rounds them.

Bear Creek Lake sits near the mouth of Bear Creek Can-yon, at the base of the foothills. The Soda Lakes, host to a variety of water-born activities, also lie within this lovely park. The well-maintained concrete and asphalt trail that loops through the park offers views and access to all these lakes, as well as picnic areas, scenic viewpoints, and other amenities.

The path is easy to follow from the outset, following the pinkish concrete path that circles up and left (south) from the parking area. Cross the park road, then pass the visitor center and views of the Soda Lakes. Head downhill past the dirt road that leads to the lakes at 0.7 mile, staying straight (southeast) on the paved path.

At 1.4 miles, you will reach a covered picnic table and interpretive sign. Beyond lie camping and picnic sites. Con-tinue straight (southeast) on the paved trail, which descends into a draw and crosses a bridge spanning Turkey Creek at 2 miles. Climb over a hill, and drop into prairie dog territory at 2.6 miles.

A meandering climb takes you above the prairie dog town toward the Mount Carbon summit, and an intersection with an asphalt trail. Stay right (east) on the concrete path, which climbs to another trail intersection. Go left, to the view-point on the summit of Mount Carbon at 3.5 miles.

After enjoying the views, backtrack down the concrete trail to the asphalt trail. Go right (down and northwest) on the asphalt trail toward Bear Creek Lake. At 4.4 miles, you will reach the lakeside trail, which runs along the top of the lower shelf of the dam, just above the water.

At 5 miles, leave the dam behind and make the gentle climb to the Mountain View overlook and parking area. Continue straight (north) past the gate to the paved park maintenance road. Turn left (west) onto the roadway, and drop to Kumpfmiller Drive, the main park road. You can follow the park road back to the trailhead, but it is much more pleasant to follow horse trails that parallel the north bank of Bear Creek to return to the parking area and trail-head.

Red Rocks and Morrison Slide Trails
Dakota Ridge Trail

16
RED ROCKS AND
MORRISON SLIDE TRAILS

Type of hike: Lollipop loop.
Total distance: 4 miles.
Elevation gain: 600 feet.
Maps: USGS Morrison; Matthews-Winters Park brochure.
Jurisdiction: Matthews-Winters Park, Jefferson County Open Space Department, and Red Rocks Park, Denver Mountain Parks Department.
Facilities: There is a small parking area at this trailhead; complete facilities, including restrooms, a water source, and a picnic area, are located in the northern section of the park.
Finding the trailhead: Take Interstate 70 west to the Morrison/Colorado 26 exit. Go left (south) on Colorado 26 for 1.5 miles to the entrance to Red Rocks Park. Drive up the paved road toward the amphitheater for 0.7 mile to where a dirt road takes off to the left (east). The trailhead is opposite the dirt road on the right (west) side of the paved park road.

Key points:
0.0 Trailhead.
1.0 Reach the junction of the Morrison Slide Trail.
2.2 Drop off of the slide to the Red Rocks Trail.
3.0 Return to the original Red Rocks/Morrison Slide Trail junction.

The hike: The towering, rosy-smooth stone edifices of the Fountain Formation, which also comprise the ramparts of the famous Red Rocks Amphitheater, are just one remarkable feature of this trail loop. Equally as impressive as passing beneath these flaming walls is the view from atop the large, flat plain of the Morrison Slide. From the summit of this jumble of now-stable rock and soil, which once was part of adjacent Mount Morrison, you can see south down the hogback valley to the famed Red Rocks Amphitheater and beyond, east over the hogback to the high plains, and north to the Table Mountains. It is high desert up on the slide, studded with yucca and cactus, but enough grass grows in the rocky soil to feed a small herd of deer, which can be seen most easily near sunrise and sunset.

To begin the hike, leave the parking area and walk north and west up the trail. Pass beneath a tall red rock overhanging a seasonal stream. At less than 0.1 mile, a Jefferson County Open Space sign marks the trail.

The path climbs beside and beneath huge red rock formations as it heads north; pass between two junipers as the trail curves to the west to the intersection of the Morrison Slide Trail and the Red Rocks Trail intersection (1 mile). Go left (northwest) on the Morrison Slide Trail, climbing six switchbacks up the face of the slide.

Lichen-encrusted rocks litter the sides of the trail as you near the top of the slide. Once you've gawked at the stupendous views from the broad flat summit, you will follow the trail as it winds along the eastern edge of the slide, then drops down steep switchbacks from its northern edge to the intersection with the Red Rocks Trail at 2.2 miles.

Turn right (east, then south) on the Red Rocks Trail, which curves around the base of the east face of the slide through the scrub of the high desert. At 3 miles, you will reach the intersection of the Red Rocks and Morrison Slide trails on the south side of the slide. From here, turn left (south and east) and retrace your steps back to the trailhead.

Option: From the northern terminus of the Morrison Slide Trail, you can turn left (north) on the Red Rocks Trail and walk 0.7 mile to the Village Walk Trail. While not as scenic as the southern portion of the hike, tucked as it is in the shadow of Interstate 70, this 1-mile trail loop offers glimpses into the history of Colorado. The trail circles the site of Mount Vernon, which briefly served as home of the governor of the Territory of Jefferson. A tiny cemetery sits west of the trail, a poignant reminder of frontier hardships.

17
DAKOTA RIDGE TRAIL

Type of hike: Out-and-back.

see map page 60

Total distance: 3.6 miles.

Elevation gain: 200 feet.

Maps: USGS Morrison; Matthews-Winters Park brochure.

Jurisdiction: Hogback Park, Jefferson County Open Space Department.

Facilities: The parking lot at the trailhead for this hike doubles as a park-n-ride lot and access to a geological walk on the hogback. More complete park facilities, including restrooms, and a picnic area, are located across Colorado 26 at Matthews-Winters Park.

Finding the trailhead: Take the Morrison/Colorado 26 exit off of Interstate 70. Go south; the parking lot is adjacent to the freeway on the southeast corner of the interchange. Park in the lot at the base of the hogback; the trailhead is at the south end of the lot.

Key points:

0.0 Trailhead.

1.8 Reach the switchbacks to West Alameda Parkway.

The hike: Hiking on the Dakota Hogback is like walking on the spine of a slumbering dinosaur—climbing steeply up its long tail to its rump, tromping down the back and up over the shoulders, then skittering down its long neck at trail's end.

The hogback, also called Dinosaur Ridge, is best known as the site of fossilized remains of prehistoric behemoths that once inhabited this area. These remains, most notably footprints, are described by interpretive signs along the Dinosaur Walk Trail on the east side of the hogback ridge, alongside West Alameda Parkway. The 2-mile long Dakota Ridge Trail does not take you to those remains. Instead, it rides the summit of the ridge and offers views of Bear Creek Lake, Soda Lakes, the hogback valley, and, on clear days, Pikes Peak, as it traverses the ancient ridge.

To begin the hike, climb southeast out of the lot onto a service road, then head left (northeast) and up on the road. Pass through a gate as you climb; at the trail marker, go right (south) and up to the crest of the ridge.

Near the ridgetop, the trail traverses through a wind-stunted pine forest. At the trail marker on the crest, the trail veers to the right (south), hooks over the ridge to its east side, and begins a rocky descent.

At about 0.7 mile, you will pass through a grassy notch in the ridge, then climb the stair-step trail back toward the crest. Pass a couple of high, open areas with views to the east and south before the trail begins to descend.

As you head gently downward, you will pass jagged rock outcrops on the right (west), then a good picnic/view area. Toward the trail's end, the path begins to drop more steeply, with good exposure as it skirts rock outcrops along the ridge.

At about 1.8 miles, go left (east) and descend two switchbacks to stairs, which drop to West Alameda Parkway and offer access to the Dinosaur Walk. Return as you came.

Meadow View and Painter's Pause Trails

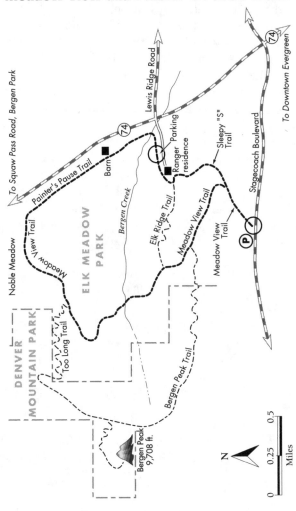

18
MEADOW VIEW AND PAINTER'S PAUSE TRAILS

Type of hike: Loop.
Total distance: 5.5 miles.
Elevation gain: 300 feet.
Maps: USGS Evergreen and Squaw Pass; Elk Meadow Park brochure.
Jurisdiction: Elk Meadow Park, Jefferson County Open Space.
Facilities: There are two trailheads and parking areas at Elk Meadow. You will find restrooms and picnic areas at both. There is also a ranger residence at the Lewis Ridge Road trailhead; contact the ranger only in case of emergency.
Finding the trailhead: To reach Elk Meadow, take Interstate 70 west to the Evergreen Parkway exit (Exit 252). Take the Evergreen Parkway (also known as Colorado 74) south for 5.3 miles to Stagecoach Boulevard. Turn right (west) on Stagecoach Boulevard, and follow it for 1.2 miles to the parking area, which is on the right (north) side of the road.

Key points:
0.0 Trailhead.
0.3 Pass the Sleepy S Trail.
1.0 The Bergen Peak Trail takes off to the left (west).
1.2 Pass the Elk Ridge Trail.
2.2 The Too Long Trail heads up Bergen Peak.
3.1 The Painter's Pause Trail begins.

4.1 Pick up the Sleepy S Trail.
5.2 Rejoin the Meadow View Trail.

The hike: Pleasant and relatively flat, this hike meanders through the meadow and forest that blankets the eastern flank of 9,708-foot Bergen Peak. The huge meadow is chameleon-like—in spring, the vibrantly green grasses are painted with swaths of yellow, pink, and purple wildflowers; in fall, the golden grasses are stained with the russets, reds, and oranges of late-season blooms and deciduous shrubs. Relatively open stands of lodgepole and ponderosa pine throughout the park are dotted with aspen.

The burgeoning community of Evergreen has encroached on the borders of this park in recent years. This has been both a curse and a blessing. The curse: The trails, which are multiuse, are often packed on sunny summer weekends, and the hum of traffic on the Evergreen Parkway precludes this as a wilderness experience. The blessing: An awareness on the part of local residents and officials of the scarcity and value of open space has resulted in the purchase of a conservation easement for Noble Meadow, a spectacular expanse of meadowland at the base of Bergen Peak's northern flanks that stretches north and east of this trail.

The Meadow View Trail begins at the northern edge of the Stagecoach parking area. Hike up past the restrooms and picnic tables; the trail arcs right (east) and traverses to the first intersection, with the Sleepy S Trail, at 0.3 mile.

Turn left (north) on the Meadow View Trail. Two switchbacks mitigate an otherwise gentle ascent to the intersection with the Bergen Peak Trail at 1 mile. Continue right (northwest) on the Meadow View Trail, which reaches the Elk Ridge Trail in a shallow saddle at 1.2 miles.

Go left (northwest) on the Meadow View Trail, dropping through a dense stand of lodgepole pines. As the path meanders along the base of Bergen Peak, it dips in and out of gullies watered by seasonal streams. You will ford these snow-fed streamlets on rocks, logs and, in one case, a rustic footbridge; the last is sheltered by a small rock grotto.

At 2.2 miles, the Too Long Trail breaks off to the left (northwest). Stay right (northeast) on the Meadow View Trail, traversing a couple of quick switchbacks that lead out of the forest and across fingers of the meadow. The footpath breaks into a doubletrack as it crowns a shallow grade, then drops into the meadow proper. Noble Meadow stretches to the north; Elk Meadow arcs east and then south, as does the trail.

You will reach the end of the Meadow View Trail near the eastern border of the park at 3.1 miles. The Painter's Pause Trail begins here, and parallels the Evergreen Parkway as it descends through the meadow, passing an old barn and crossing the marshland along Bergen Creek.

The Painter's Pause Trail ends at the Sleepy S Trail at 4.1 miles. Turn right (west) on the Sleepy S Trail, and climb past the intersection with the spur trail for the Lewis Ridge Road parking area. Continue up on Sleepy S Trail to the trail intersection at the base of the Elk Ridge Trail at 4.6 miles. Go left (southwest) on the Sleepy S Trail, which climbs through a ponderosa parkland to its end at the Meadow View Trail at 5.2 miles. Turn left (southwest) on the Meadow View Trail, and retrace your steps for 0.3 mile back to the Stagecoach Road Trailhead.

19
CHIEF MOUNTAIN

Type of hike: Out-and-back.
Total distance: 3 miles.
Elevation gain: 100 feet.
Maps: USGS Idaho Springs and Squaw Pass.
Jurisdiction: Arapaho National Forest.
Facilities: There is limited parking in a pullout on the north side of Colorado 103.
Finding the trailhead: Take Interstate 70 west to the Evergreen Parkway/Colorado 74 exit (Exit 252). Follow the Evergreen Parkway south for about 3 miles, through Bergen Park, to the stoplight at Squaw Pass Road. Turn right (west) on Squaw Pass Road, which leads to Echo Lake and Mount Evans. Follow this road, which becomes Colorado 103, west from Bergen Park for about 12 miles, and look for a pullout on the north side of CO 103. Neither the trailhead nor the parking area are marked, which can make for some confusion. You may be able to spy the decrepit orange lift towers of the old Squaw Pass Ski Area down the slope from the parking area; you may also notice mile marker 19. The more well-defined parking area for Old Squaw Pass Road is 0.4 mile east on CO 103. The trail begins by a metal stake on the south side of the road, and switchbacks up the embankment to a small white post marked "290."

Chief Mountain

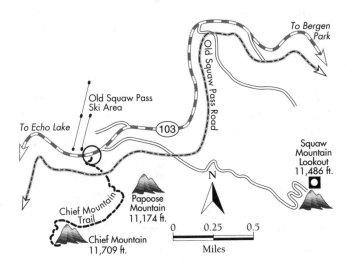

Key points:

0.0 Trailhead.

0.5 Reach the saddle between Chief Mountain and Papoose Mountain.

1.5 Arrive on the summit.

The hike: To the west rises the Continental Divide. Mount Evans looms to the southwest, gentle and comforting, like a big, white-shouldered grandpa. Southward, beyond the green summits of the lesser mountains, the distinctive cone of Pike's Peak is etched against the sky; to the north are the silvery flanks of Longs Peak. And to the east, the high plains stretch away, looking remarkably like a vast sea of green and gold.

Marginal poetry, no doubt, but this hike is truly inspirational. On a cloudless day, the views from the summit of 11,709-foot Chief Mountain rival those from atop of any of Colorado's famed 14,000-foot peaks.

The trail is a steady climb, but because it is fairly short, it qualifies as easy. Take your time, and recognize that the thinning air will slow your progress. Bring plenty of water. Pack extra clothing as well, as it can be blustery on the summit.

Begin by climbing two switchbacks up the embankment on the south side of CO 103, passing the trail post marked "290." Once in the woods, you will pass a USDA Forest Service information sign, then you will cross Old Squaw Pass Road, which runs parallel to the newer highway and offers year-round recreational opportunities (see the Options at the end of this hike description).

The Chief Mountain Trail continues on the south side of Old Squaw Pass Road in a dense lodgepole, and spruce/fir forest. Climb steadily to the saddle between Chief Mountain (on the west) and Papoose Mountain (on the east), which is at about the 0.5 mile-mark.

Climb a switchback, and circle to the north face of Chief Mountain. Above, you will break out of the woods onto the alpine tundra of the summit knob. From the vista point on a rock outcrop north of the trail, there are great views of the Continental Divide.

A series of switchbacks lead up across the gneiss rock that litters the tundra. At the east shoulder of the mountain, pass a unique rock formation at a switchback. Hike up the east face, passing through a stunted forest of bristlecone pine and subalpine fir.

A high saddle lies just below the summit, between two rock outcrops. The north (right-hand) outcrop is the summit. Scramble to the top at 1.5 miles, and bask in brilliant sunlight, the views of the surrounding summits, and the invigorating feeling found only on a mountaintop.

Head down the way you came.

Option: Old Squaw Pass Road, which runs parallel to CO 103 for more than 4 miles, offers both spectacular views of the Continental Divide to the west and the peace of a high-country forest. The road is suitable for hiking, mountain biking, and cross-country skiing, as well as motorized recreational vehicles, and offers access to numerous other Forest Service roads in the vicinity. The most obvious is the road that leads up Squaw Mountain, the balding summit east of Chief Mountain that is crowned with radio towers and an abandoned lookout. If you wish to avoid structures of civilization—especially those that hum and crackle—stick to the lower roadway, or hike up Chief Mountain.

20
APEX GULCH LOOP

Type of hike: Lollipop loop.
Total distance: 4.2 miles.
Elevation gain: 960 feet.
Maps: USGS Morrison; Apex Park brochure.
Jurisdiction: Apex Park, Jefferson County Open Space Department.
Facilities: There are ample parking spaces and restroom facilities at the trailhead.
Finding the trailhead: Take Interstate 70 west to the Morrison exit and go north, toward the Table Mountains and the city of Golden. Head north for 1.1 miles on U.S. Highway 40 to its intersection with Jefferson County 93, which is about 0.2 mile northeast of the Heritage Square complex. A quick jog north onto Jefferson County 93 lands you at the park entrance. Turn left (west) to enter the parking lot.

Key points:
0.8 Reach the Pick 'N Sledge Trail junction.
1.7 Pass the Grubstake Trail.
2.3 Head down toward the creek on the Sluicebox Trail.
2.6 Reach the creek in Apex Gulch.

The hike: This loop is illustrative of the complex interface between the urban corridor and the relative wild of the foothills of the Rocky Mountains. It begins on the edge of a

Apex Gulch Loop

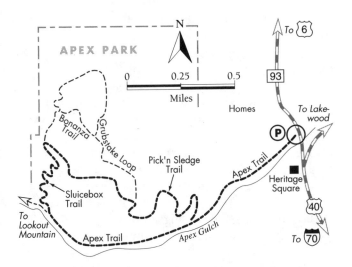

dense subdivision, complete with lawns and swingsets; Heritage Square, a popular amusement park and shopping area is to the south. As you climb up the east-facing flank of the Front Range, the city and its suburbs spread eastward like a concrete blanket. But as you crest the mountain, signs of civilization give way to a pristine ponderosa parkland, complete with beds of colorful wildflowers and an abundance of songbirds.

At the western border of the park, it is civilization again, this time in the form of a mountain subdivision. But as you drop into Apex Gulch, nature takes over again, filtering out the sights of man's handiwork with a shimmering riparian curtain, and drowning the sounds of the city with the tinkling of the creek.

The frontier history of the gulch trail is interesting, too—the Apex and Gregory Wagon Road, which runs up Apex Gulch, the centerpiece of the park, once led miners west to the gold mines of Central City and Black Hawk.

Leave the lot west through the cottonwoods, crossing a footbridge. Stay on the Apex Trail (follow the signs); a subdivision is on your right (north). Pass through a large open area to the toll road sign at the mouth of Apex Gulch. Follow the creek west to the first trail crossing; turn right (north) on the Pick 'N Sledge Trail at 0.8 mile.

Traverse northward along the dry, cacti-pocked east face on Pick 'N Sledge Trail to a series of switchbacks that climb to the Grubstake Trail crossing at 1.7 miles. Continue left (west) on Pick 'N Sledge as it climbs up toward Indian Mountain.

The trail meanders through a pine forest, then crosses the summit meadow, before heading down through open woods to the Sluicebox Trail crossing at 2.3 miles. Head down and left (south) on the Sluicebox Trail.

Eleven switchbacks land you streamside, at the junction with the Apex Trail. Go left (east) on Apex Trail at 2.6 miles.

Wander along the creek on the Apex Trail to its intersection with the Pick 'N Sledge Trail at 3.3 miles. From here, retrace your steps east to the trailhead.

21
FOREST AND MEADOW LOOP

Type of hike: Double loop.
Total distance: 1.3 miles.
Elevation gain: 120 feet.
Maps: USGS Morrison and Evergreen.
Jurisdiction: Lookout Mountain Park, Jefferson County Open Space Department.
Facilities: There is ample parking, as well as restrooms and water sources, at the trailhead. Be sure to visit the Lookout Mountain Nature Center, and the Boettcher Mansion, which may be rented for social and business events.
Finding the trailhead: To reach the conference center, take Interstate 70 west to the Lookout Mountain exit (Exit 256). Turn left (west) onto U.S. Highway 40, and go 3.5 miles to Lookout Mountain Road. Go right (east) on Lookout Mountain Road for 1.5 miles to a left (northeast) turn onto Colorow Road. Follow Colorow Road for 1.1 miles to the entrance to the conference and nature center.

Key points:
0.0 Trailhead.
0.1 Reach the unmarked trail intersection.
0.3 Enter the meadow.
1.0 Reach the Y intersection.

Forest and Meadow Loop
Beaver Brook Trail

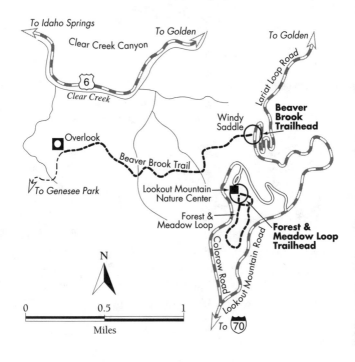

To Idaho Springs
To Golden
To Golden

Clear Creek Canyon

6

Clear Creek

Lariat Loop Road

Beaver
Brook
Trailhead

Windy
Saddle

Overlook

Beaver Brook Trail

To Genesee Park

Lookout Mountain
Nature Center

Forest &
Meadow Loop

Forest &
Meadow Loop
Trailhead

Colorow Road

Lookout Mountain Road

To 70

N

0   0.5   1
Miles

The hike: This short, educational hike, which meanders through meadow and ponderosa forest atop Lookout Mountain, offers wonderful views of the high plains and Denver, as well as comprehensive interpretation of the area's natural and cultural features.

The new Lookout Mountain Nature Center serves as the jumping-off spot for the hike; it offers interpretive programs for both the young and old (the nearby Boettcher Mansion serves as a conference center). Signs along this easy trail describe the ecology of montane wildlands.

Depart from the information kiosk on the south side of the Boettcher Mansion. At the first trail crossing, go right (west) through the ponderosa.

At the unmarked trail intersection at 0.1 mile, go left (west) on the Forest Loop. Don't fret the lack of trail signs—all trails loop back to the nature center. Cross the bridge and take the right (northerly) fork onto the Meadow Loop at about 0.3 mile. Panoramic views of the plains open up as the trail enters the meadow.

A stone chimney rises on the left (north) side of the trail, then the path passes through a small grove of quaking aspen. The trail curves around the west end of the meadow and heads east through waist-high grasses. The panorama of Denver and the high plains is spread before you.

At about the 1-mile mark, you will pass through a small pine grove. The trail splits in a Y intersection; go right (east) into the ponderosa parkland. Cross a footbridge and begin a gentle ascent through the trees.

Return to the first trail crossing on the south side of the mansion; bear right (east) to the kiosk and parking lot.

22
BEAVER BROOK TRAIL

Type of hike: Out-and-back.

see map page 78

Total distance: About 3 miles.
Elevation gain: 240 feet.
Maps: USGS Morrison and Evergreen.
Jurisdiction: Denver Mountain Parks Department.
Facilities: There is a small parking area at Windy Saddle, but no restrooms or water sources are available.
Finding the trailhead: To reach the Windy Saddle trailhead, take Interstate 70 west to the Lookout Mountain exit (Exit 256). Turn left (west) onto U.S. Highway 40, and go 3.5 miles to Lookout Mountain Road. Go right (east) on Lookout Mountain Road, which becomes the Lariat Loop Road, for 4.4 miles. The trailhead and parking area are well-marked on the west side of Lariat Loop Road.

Key points:
0.0 Trailhead.
0.1 Pass the Lookout Mountain Trail intersection; the trail is designated for hiking only beyond this point.
1.0 Reach the first open area.
1.5 Arrive at the overlook.

The hike: Because of its scenic qualities and lengthy history at the forefront of Front Range hiking trails, the venerable

Beaver Brook Trail is one of the most popular trails in the area. The relatively level trail—except for some dramatic elevation gains and losses on the westernmost end—winds near the summit of the southern flank of Clear Creek Canyon for about 8.5 miles to Genesee Park. Depending on time and commitment, you can do as much of it as you like. The easternmost 1.5 miles, described here, offer a taste of what you will see along the route.

Look to the sky—it is not uncommon to see hawks and eagles riding the thermals. Look to the west, where the white-capped Continental Divide thrusts skyward. Look below, at the silver thread of Clear Creek as it winds through the steep canyon it has carved.

This is not a trail for the faint-hearted. In places, the drop from the narrow path into the canyon is precipitous; in other places, hands-on scrambling over rock outcrops is necessary. Bring good shoes and leave the very small at home.

Depart west from Windy Saddle. Views to the east, which you can enjoy more on the return trip, are of South Table Mountain; to the west is the steep chasm of Clear Creek Canyon. The views are lost quickly, however, as the trail enters the woods and begins to climb. At the Lookout Mountain Trail crossing at about 0.1 mile, go right (west) on the Beaver Brook Trail.

The section of trail between this intersection and the first open area to the west is the most challenging. Begin by crossing two small-scale spills of talus, staying to the uphill side of both. The trail passes between two boulders, then meanders along a hillside to a series of three rock scrambles. At about one-half mile, cross a gully carved by a seasonal stream. The trail ascends beneath a steep rock face; there is thrilling exposure here. Stay high where the trail appears to fork.

The trail crosses above a rock slide, drops into a wooded gully, then descends over a series of rock outcrops before spilling into an open, grassy area at about 1 mile. Pause here to enjoy views of the plains and the Table Mountains to the east, and the canyon to the north.

The next 0.5 mile leads through a section of woods to a flat shady area near a seasonal stream. Pass through a tunnel of pine and juniper trees to a rolling meadow. A flat-topped rock outcrop juts out over the canyon just west of the meadow at about 1.5 miles; from the trail near this landmark, you can enjoy great vistas north and west into Clear Creek Canyon and to the Continental Divide. Remain on the trail, as straying may lead you onto private land.

After taking in the sights, head back the way you came.

Option: As mentioned above, this trail continues for about 7 miles to the Chief Hosa area near Evergreen. Hike as much further as you please. Plan a long day to do a round-trip tour, or arrange to have a shuttle pick you up at the western terminus of the trail, which is located off Stapleton Drive in Genesee Park.

23
MAVERICK AND SAWMILL TRAILS

Type of hike: Loop.
Total distance: 2.4 miles.
Elevation gain: 280 feet.
Maps: USGS Ralston Buttes; White Ranch Park Map.
Jurisdiction: White Ranch Park, Jefferson County Open Space.
Facilities: There is ample parking, restrooms, picnic shelters, and a ranger residence (contact the ranger only in emergencies) at the trailhead.
Finding the trailhead: Take Interstate 70 to the Morrison exit (Exit 259). Go right (north) on U.S. Highway 40 for 1.1 miles to Jefferson County 93. Jog onto CR 93, and go 1.1 miles to U.S. Highway 6. Turn left (north), and follow US 6 to its intersection with Colorado 93 and Colorado 58. Go straight (north) on CO 93 for 1.8 miles to Golden Gate Canyon Road. Turn left (west) and go 3.9 miles to Crawford Gulch Road. Turn right (north) on Crawford Gulch Road, traveling 4 miles to Belcher Hill Road. Turn right (east), and go 1.8 miles to the parking lot and trailhead.

Key points:
0.3 Reach the Longhorn Trail.
0.7 Arrive at the Maverick Trail intersection.
1.6 Reach the Sawmill Trail.

Maverick and Sawmill Trails

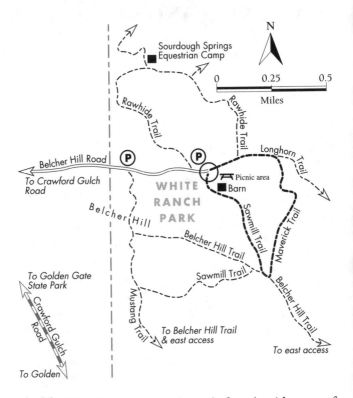

The hike: The high plains wash out before the ridgetops of the Front Range like an ocean of green and brown. No doubt it was from vantage points as broad and far-seeing as those along the Maverick Trail that Ute and Arapaho Indians surveyed the awesome prairie for the dark stain of buffalo. And no doubt the homesteaders that settled these high-country meadows also marveled at the vast scope of the grasslands. Likewise, the eyes of the modern hiker will be drawn eastward to marvel at the beauty of the high plains, glistening with its patchwork overlay of the handiwork of humankind.

The scope and variation of the wildlands within this park, which host more than 18 miles of trail, demand exploration. This trail loop has a frontier feel, beginning and ending near the old ranch that was part of Paul R. White's homestead.

To begin this loop, head east out of the parking lot toward the picnic areas and restrooms. The high plains are spread before you, with the Table Mountains decorating the southeast horizon, and the striking redness of the Ralston Buttes rising to the northeast.

At 0.3 mile, pick up the Longhorn Trail, which passes through a parkland of ponderosa pines as it heads gently downward. Descend a switchback to the Maverick Trail at 0.7 mile. Go right (southeast) on the Maverick Trail.

Pass rock outcrops as the trail curves into a draw. Cross the creek and climb up the wooded slope. From the crest of the hill, the trail heads southwest over rolling grass and wildflower-coated terrain.

The Maverick Trail deadends at Belcher Hill Trail; turn right (northwest) for less than 0.1 mile to the Sawmill Trail at 1.6 miles. Go right (north) on the Sawmill Trail.

The Sawmill Trail bends northwest as it approaches, then follows a fence that corrals a red barn and other ranch buildings. Pass another trail sign and continue through the meadow toward the parking area. You will arrive back at the parking area and trailhead at the 2.4-mile mark.

Mule Deer, Coyote, and Elk Trails

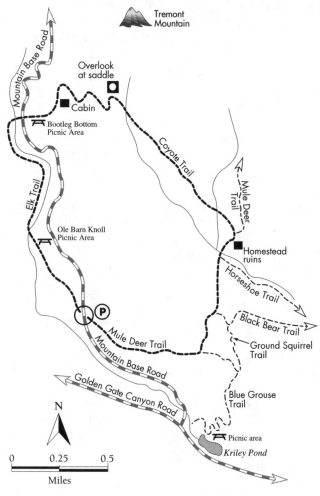

24
MULE DEER, COYOTE, AND ELK TRAILS

Type of hike: Loop.
Total distance: 5.5 miles.
Elevation gain: 1000 feet.
Maps: USGS Black Hawk; Golden Gate Canyon State Park trail map.
Jurisdiction: Golden Gate Canyon State Park.
Facilities: There is nothing but parking available at the trailhead, but the park has ample facilities, including restrooms, a visitor and nature center, and campgrounds. There is a $4 fee for a daily vehicle pass; annual passes are $40.
Finding the trailhead: From the intersection of US Highway 6 and Colorado 93, go north on CO 93 for 1.8 miles to Golden Gate Canyon Road. Turn left (west), following the canyon road 13 miles to the park entrance. At the intersection with Crawford Gulch Road near the visitor center, go left (west) on Golden Gate Canyon Road for 1.3 miles to Mountain Base Road. Turn right (northeast) on Mountain Base Road, and go 0.9 mile to the trailhead on the left (west) side of the road.

Key points:
0.0 Trailhead.
1.5 Reach Frazer Meadow and the Coyote Trail.
4.2 Reach Bootleg Bottom and the Elk Trail.
5.0 Pass the Ole Barn Knoll picnic area.
5.5 Return to the trailhead.

The hike: This trail pushes the parameters of an easy hike, but it does so in exhilarating ways, taking you into the backcountry that makes Colorado so special, and immersing you in remarkable vistas and soothing seclusion.

Start the hike on the east side of Mountain Base Road, picking up the Mule Deer Trail, which ascends into the woods, intersecting the Blue Grouse Trail at about 0.2 mile. Continue left (northeast) on the Mule Deer Trail.

Pass a level section of trail at about 1 mile. At the intersection with the Horseshoe Trail, stay left (northeast) on the Mule Deer Trail. At about 1.5 miles, the trail descends into Frazer Meadow. Pass the old homestead; the trail veers right (north) to the Coyote Trail. Take the Coyote Trail left (northwest), skirting the eastern edge of the broad, colorful meadow.

The valley narrows as the trail ascends along the flanks of Tremont Mountain, and climbs around broad switchbacks. The steepening climb ends at a rocky saddle at about 2.5 miles. Views west are of the Indian Peaks.

Descend west from the saddle, rounding several switchbacks through a dense woodland. The trail curves through a clear-cut, then passes an old log cabin. Follow the logging track to where the trail veers off left (south), crossing a gully. Beyond the second gully, you will enter the picnic grounds at Bootleg Bottom at the 4.2-mile mark.

Continue west on Coyote Trail across Mountain Base Road. At the Elk Trail intersection, turn left and head south on the Elk Trail. Drop gently through the meadow to the Ole Barn Knoll Trail intersection and picnic area at 5 miles. From the picnic area, the Elk Trail continues south, kicking over the toe of a knoll to the trailhead at 5.5 miles.